POLAR BEAR

POLAR BEAR

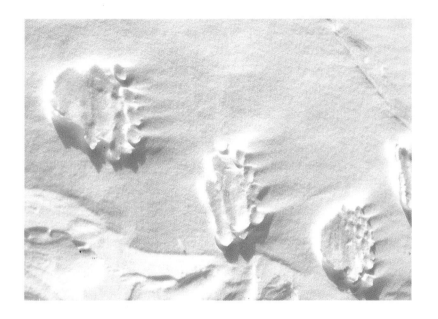

Photography by Dan Guravich

Text by Downs Matthews

CHRONICLE BOOKS

SAN FRANCISCO

Printed in Japan.
Book and cover design: Gail Grant

Library of Congress Cataloging in Publication Data
Guravich, Dan.
    Polar bear / photographs by Dan Guravich ; text by Downs Matthews.
        p.   cm.
    ISBN 0-8118-0050-X
    ISBN 0-8118-0204-3 (pbk.)
    1. Polar bear. 2. Polar bear—Pictorial works. I. Matthews. Downs. II. Title.
QL737.C27G87 1993
599.74'446—dc20   92-46355
                                                                    CIP

Distributed in Canada
by Raincoast Books,
112 East Third Avenue, Vancouver, B.C. V5T 1C8

10 9 8 7 6 5 4 3 2 1

Chronicle Books
275 Fifth Street
San Francisco, CA 94103

Captions for front pages:

Title: Snow compressed by a polar bear's weight remains in place while surrounding loose snow is blown away by the wind, leaving behind a raised impression of the footprints.

Dedication: Polar bear mothers give birth to their cubs in den sites selected for concealment and for proximity to the sea, so that they don't have far to travel to resume hunting for seals.

Facing Contents: In white-out conditions, when visibility is reduced to 20 feet or less, polar bears rely on their superb sense of smell to detect the presence of food or other animals.

To Ursus maritimus, *a noble animal, often misunderstood, maligned, and persecuted, who deserves better of mankind.*

Contents

Creatures of the twilight, polar bears may hunt, sleep, play, or move about at any hour of night or day.

A Passion for Polar Bears: Preface

Dan Guravich

In 60 years as a photographer and biologist, I have never found a subject more compelling, more satisfying, than that of polar bears. Personally, I find nothing exceptional about that. But when others learn of my interest, they usually express amazement or skepticism, especially when I tell them that I live in Greenville, Mississippi.

Of course, my passion for polar bears didn't originate in the Deep South, but in the Far North.

For one thing, I am a Canadian, born in Winnipeg, Manitoba, a province famous for its polar bears. My interest in photography began as a childhood hobby and grew steadily until, as a geneticist with the United States Department of Agriculture assigned to a cotton research station in Greenville, I discovered that it was possible to make a living as a location photographer.

I encountered my first wild polar bear in his natural habitat when serving as official photographer aboard the SS *Manhattan* during her historic voyage through the Northwest Passage in 1968. Eight years later, given a magazine assignment to photograph polar bears, I journeyed to Churchill on the shores of Hudson Bay, where polar bears congregate each fall. There I met Len Smith, a mechanical genius. At my suggestion, Len contrived a Tundra Buggy in which we might transport ourselves and our gear onto the frozen tundra for weeks of observing polar bears up close. I became so thoroughly charmed with the magnificent animals that I began to welcome the arrival of fall with the eager anticipation one normally reserves for a dear old friend.

From one side of the Arctic to the other, I have followed my white-furred brothers, watching, listening, and photographing, but mostly, enjoying. I've shared the love of a starving mother as she suckled her two cubs; I've felt the joy of young bears as they played together in the snow; I've suffered anguish over the death of a cub in the jaws of a predatory male. I have followed closely the growing scientific understanding of the species, and I have lamented the killing of polar bears by so-called hunters and the mistreatment of bears by insensitive researchers.

In short, my focus on polar bears has sharpened my appreciation of the entire natural world. To my way of thinking, there is no animal anywhere, including those of the great plains of Africa, more deserving of man's admiration and more worthy of his protection. In these pages, Downs Matthews and I have sought not only to examine a fascinating species in intimate detail but to convey a sense of the respect and affection that we have come to feel for the polar bear. I hope that you, too, will be similarly persuaded that the lords of the Arctic have few peers in the kingdom of the animals.

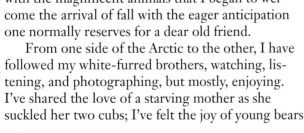

Right: In the wild, 20 years is a long life for a polar bear, although one may live up to 40 years in captivity.

Polar Bear People: Introduction

Next time the television weather reporter shows you a map of North America, look for Hudson Bay, that large, pear-shaped body of water that lies north of the Great Lakes between the Canadian provinces of Manitoba and Quebec. On the bay's western shore, about halfway down, note the shelf of land that juts eastward about 40 miles from the town of Churchill. English explorers named the tip of that promontory Cape Churchill. Eskimos who sometimes hunted there called it Land of the Polar Bears. In recent years, it might also be known as the Land of the Polar Bear People.

Each autumn, polar bear admirers gather here, traveling from around the world to arrive with the season's first snows. They come to watch, photograph, and enjoy the polar bears that gather by the score on Cape Churchill where a unique combination of geography and circumstances brings people and arctic wildlife together.

While most of the High Arctic's polar bears remain on sea ice throughout the year, those of Hudson Bay are forced ashore in summer when the bay ice melts. Without pack ice on which to hunt the ringed and bearded seals on which they live, the bears can only wait near the water's edge for winter to return and freeze the bay, allowing them to hunt once again.

When the chill winds of October herald on-coming winter, the Churchill bears take notice. For three months they have fasted, living on stored body fat. Encouraged by the deepening cold, they begin moving north toward the advancing sea ice. Some fetch up on Cape Churchill itself, the point where the Hudson Bay ice pack will first close with the land-fast ice on which they wait.

November on Cape Churchill brings subzero temperatures. Fierce gales hurl powdery snow

through the dry air, forming aerodynamic shapes in the lees of diminutive flag trees and rocky hummocks. Leaden clouds pass through, taking their load of flaky white "termination dust" south. Each day, the band of open salt water between the expanding ice pack and the shore becomes narrower. Slowly the slush congeals and the glare ice hardens. A couple of weeks of exposure to 10-below-zero cold will thicken the ice sufficiently to allow polar bears to roam freely over it in search of seals.

That's when the Tundra Buggies roll east from the little town of Churchill, laden with people who find wildlife and wilderness far more captivating and satisfying than all the cathedrals and museums of the civilized world. Under the direction of Len Smith, who built them, the safari of four motorized vehicles, two bunk houses, a dining car, and a utility trailer sets up camp on the bed of a frozen lake in the sheltering lee of the Cape Churchill esker. There, Dr. Dan Guravich, whose photographs illustrate this book, takes charge. As a biologist and wildlife photographer, he has made nearly 50 trips to the Arctic. His knowledge of polar bears is exceeded only by his appreciation for them. He is joined by up to 32 people, all agog at the presence of bears.

In a buggy parked by the shore, its engine stilled, Guravich scans the ice that lies in a jack-straw jumble in the tidal zone. With his practiced eye, he soon spots *Ursus maritimus* in his native land. An off-white on white, a bear plods farmerlike across his frozen field. A mature male, he is hunting the edge of the land-fast ice for an unwary seal.

With the glad smile one reserves for an old friend, Guravich raises a window and opens a can of sardines. The bear stops. His head swivels toward the source of the aroma as if he had an olfactory compass in his nose. Capable of smelling a few

molecules of scent at a distance of 20 miles, he enjoys a rich sensory experience at 100 yards.

Clearly, sardine is not an hors d'oeuvre with which this bear is familiar. Seal blubber would bring him running. A young walrus would make his mouth water. Beluga whale would be a welcome treat. But this white giant is hungry, and something that smells this good must be investigated.

The bear rises to his big square feet and plods over the icy clutter to the vehicle.

Guravich cautions his photographers. No talking. No sudden moves. Don't alarm the visitor who has come to investigate this large white sardine can on wheels.

At a distance of 10 yards, the world's largest non-aquatic carnivore stops and sits again to contemplate us. Although he can run as fast as a mile in two minutes, he doesn't like to rush into things. He's a splendid young male, seven years old and weighing about 800 pounds. His neck and face are unblemished, as yet unscarred by the mating wars that await him next spring. Though sexually mature, he also has yet to reach the fighting weight of 1,000 to 1,200 pounds that will enable him to win the brief but ferocious battles in which males compete for females.

Rays of the feeble morning sun radiate like a golden halo from his thick pelage. The hollow hairs of his coat transmit warmth to the black skin beneath. A three-inch layer of blubber encases his body, insulating him against the severest cold. Sharp, curved black claws fringe his hair-mantled feet to give him purchase on slippery surfaces. His long neck and powerful hindquarters provide the leverage to yank a 700-pound bearded seal through a breathing hole and onto the ice. Nanuk, as the Eskimos call him, is the consummate Arctic predator. ("Eskimo" is the name used here and used commonly among the native people who live across polar bear regions of Canada, Alaska, and Siberia, and who also go by geographically differentiated names such as Inuit in Canada and Inupiat in Alaska.)

Having never encountered anything to fear in his monochrome world, the *Eismeister* decides to inspect us more closely. More curious than aggressive, he approaches the vehicle and with a sudden, fluid movement, rises to his full 10-foot height. He places his front paws on the side of the vehicle and peers in a window. His wet black nose flexes and his small brown eyes stare as he records the smell and look of these strange creatures. His heavily furred ears cock forward to capture the curious sounds that emanate from within this igloo on wheels.

Our reactions cut across the psychological spectrum. One of the eight people in our buggy shrinks

Left: Classified by taxonomists as a marine mammal, the polar bear is as much at home in water as on land.

Below: To a polar bear it is always nap time, and any surface will serve as a bed.

away with a gasp of fear. Another leans toward the bear and croons baby talk. A third, mouth hanging open, is struck dumb and cannot move. From the inner recesses of our atavistic souls, the thought surfaces that we are small, helpless creatures caught out of our trees by a meat-eater as efficient and hungry as any dire wolf or saber-toothed tiger.

But the buggy's high metal sides shield us and confidence returns. Guravich grins a welcome. "Hello, there," he chirps. "How are you?" Although he has seen thousands of polar bears up close, his pleasure in them remains fresh and keen. "They are the most exciting and beautiful of all of nature's children," he says.

Creatures of the Glacial Epoch, polar bears came recently into the animal world. Zoologists believe the sea bear evolved about 250,000 years ago from brown-bear ancestors that had learned to feed on the bounteous prey base of marine mammals populating the circumpolar north.

Summer in the Arctic brings endless days when the sun plays touch and go with the horizon. Winter in contrast, brings endless nights, when the sun's presence is betrayed only by a vague lightening of the eastern sky. Science describes the polar bear as a "crepuscular" animal, one that becomes active in the twilight of morning or night. But in practice the presence or absence of light seems immaterial to a polar bear. In a world of endless days or endless nights, the polar bear must meet his needs when they arise, whatever the hour.

Aside from a fondness for sleep and a passion for eating, polar bears share a compelling curiosity about anything that enters their hostile environment. Given the opportunity, a polar bear will find a way into any house, cache, or vehicle and having examined the contents, attempt to eat whatever he can get his teeth around.

One day at Cape Churchill, Dan Guravich noticed a young male bear shredding and eating what looked like blue cloth. As the Churchill campers take great pains to discard nothing onto the ice, Guravich became concerned, wondering what the bear had found and where he had found it. Closer examination revealed that the item was a pair of blue jeans, and what's more, they were his. Guravich had placed some extra jeans, a pair of dress shoes, and a pair of down-filled wind pants in a small bag, which he had stored in a corner of a utility trailer attached to the bunk house. Somehow, the bear had patiently forced a hole between the trailer's wooden slats, and inserting his muzzle, had snared the bag. He pulled it out, opened it up, ate the shoes for starters, and was working on the jeans. He had set the wind pants aside, presumably as dessert. Hoping to save the expensive wind pants, Guravich tried to distract the bear with yells and loud noises. But the youngster was enjoying his meal and paid no attention. Finally, when the bear turned his attention to the wind pants, Guravich seized upon a pan of freshly baked muffins. As the bear began to nibble the pants, Guravich threw him a muffin. Charmed, the bear sniffed, licked, and after several minutes, ate the muffin. When he turned back to the wind pants, Guravich threw him another muffin. For two hours, using 18 bran muffins, Guravich kept the bear amused and his wind pants intact. As the last muffin was thrown, one of the Tundra Buggies returned to camp. The bear moved off and the buggy driver was able to hop down and retrieve the pants.

Similarly, curiosity was the motive that professional pilot Harry Hanlan assigned to an unexpected visit from a polar bear on Ellesmere Island. While waiting for a flight to arrive in the Calgary, Alberta, airport, he told me his favorite bear story.

"I flew a Twin Otter into Okse Bay to check on a trailer that had been used by geologists during the 1970s," Hanlan recalls. "They had stored food supplies and camping gear in it. We landed on a gravel bar and walked 500 yards to the trailer. It had been plundered by bears. Their tracks were all over the place, some of them fresh. They had broken out the windows and had dragged out everything within reach of their claws and jaws. There was bedding, clothing, furniture, and food in cans and boxes scattered all over the place. We tried to take an inventory, but something warned me to leave. So we started back to the airplane. About halfway there, I looked back and saw a polar bear about 200 yards away and running toward us. We ran to the plane and got in. The bear trotted up to us, but when it got there, it just sat down and watched. We started the engines and revved them up but the bear didn't move. Not until we began taxiing the plane did it saunter off, still watching us. It never attempted to harm us in any way, and I think it was just curious about what we were up to. But we didn't wait to find out."

Bears exhibit other emotions, as well, sometimes venting anger at a mistake or disappointment.

While Dr. Ian Stirling, Canada's leading polar bear zoologist, was observing bear behavior out on the ice, he saw a polar bear mistake a 10-gallon steel drum for a seal. The bear stalked it with skill and care, creeping up quietly for the better part of an hour. Finally, the bear pounced and discovered his mistake. When he saw what he had caught, he "gave it a cuff that sent it spinning several meters across the ice."

Bear hunter Warren Matumeak of Barrow, Alaska, reports a bear's reaction to missing an easy meal. The bear invested much time and effort in stalking a ringed seal on the ice. "He got close," Matumeak says, "and made a dash for it, but the seal got away. The bear was so annoyed with itself and disappointed that he kicked the snow and slapped the ice in irritation."

Accounts of 18th and 19th century explorers of the Arctic report human contact with polar bears, many of which occurred when the bear swam to meet their ship or walked right into camp. Often, the visitors were killed by gunfire and eaten. But the United States Grinnell Expedition of 1850, while searching for the lost party of Sir John Franklin, made a mess of its first bear encounter. Dr. Elisha Kent Kane reported it in his diary, published in 1856.

The bear "was not the sleepy thing which, with begrimed hair and dirty face, appeals to your sympathies as he walks the endless rounds of a wet cage. Our first polar bear moved past us on the floes with the leisurely march of fearless freedom. . . . He reminded us of a colossal puss in boots."

Chasing the bear, "we were an absurd party of zealots, rushing pell-mell upon the floes with vastly more energy than discretion. While walking in the lightest manner over the suspicious ice, my companion next in line . . . disappeared, gun and all; yet, after getting him out, we insanely continued our chase with the aid of boats. After laboring very hard for about three hours, repeated duckings in water at 30 degrees cooled down our enthusiasm. The bear, meantime, never varied from his unconcerned walk. We saw him last in a labyrinth of hummock ice."

At one time, it was thought that polar bears were migrants, Gypsies of the ice, constantly on the move. In actuality, polar bears tend to stay near the area of their birth. Scientists have identified 12 subpopulations among an estimated 40,000 polar bears that range the frozen waters of the United States, Canada, Denmark, Norway, and Russia. The number of bears in each subpopulation rises or falls or

Facing page: An active polar bear quickly becomes overheated and must take steps to cool off. While capable of running a mile in two minutes, a polar bear cannot run that far at that speed without becoming seriously stressed by heat.

nomenon the Arctic Ring of Life, because of the great number of marine mammals it sustains.

Human populations were similarly sustained in the Far North. Scientists suggest that as long ago as 30,000 years, nomadic hunters prowled through the region known as the Arctic, following the migrations of game animals now extinct, such as the wooly mammoth and the mastodon. Between 5,000 and 3,000 years ago, ancestral Eskimos began developing a technology enabling them to specialize successfully in the hunting of seal, walrus, whale, polar bear, and the smaller animals of the arctic ecosystem. They created what is called the Arctic Small Tool tradition, and they took their skills to the barren lands bordering the Ring of Life.

Following them came the peoples known today under the convenient rubric of Eskimo, which translates as "eaters of raw meat." Around 1000 B.C., the ancestors of today's Eskimo peoples moved out of North America's interior. They began to displace those of the Arctic Small Tool tradition by virtue of still-superior technology for maritime hunting. Traveling over the sea ice by dog sled in winter and across the water by kayak in summer, they eventually occupied the lands of the Arctic.

For these latterday Eskimos, the polar bear had magical significance as a close relative as well as a powerful and worthy adversary. One myth held that polar bears once were a race of humans, but became bears by dressing themselves in fur. In their igloos, the bears would take off their skins and become people again. When an Eskimo woman discovered their secret, they became furious and sought to kill her and every Eskimo since.

Across the dreadful ice came monstrous and magical polar bears such as Kuqqugiaq, a huge beast with ten legs that preyed upon people. In Point Barrow, Alaska, Warren Matumeak recalled the

remains stable depending largely on the availability of the seals on which they live. Canada probably leads the world in numbers of polar bears with an estimated 20,000 animals prowling the ice around the barren islands of the Canadian Archipelago.

Recent research by wildlife zoologists of the United States and Russia suggests that the polar bears of Alaska's Beaufort Sea and those of Siberia's Chukchi Sea are actually members of the same population. Many, perhaps most, of the bears seen off the North Slope of Alaska, Russian experts say, were probably born on Wrangel Island. There, 500 birth dens, the world's densest concentration, have been mapped.

While polar bears are identified with the North Pole, they are seldom found in the deep interior of the Arctic known as the Polar Basin. Instead, they congregate along the perimeter of the polar ice pack where ocean currents break apart the ice and create leads of open water called polynyas. Seals surface in these polynyas, and their year-round presence attracts bears eager to feed on them. Russian biologist Savva Uspenski named this circumpolar phe-

legend of an ancestor who thought of a way to kill Kuqqugiaq. When attacked, the hunter speared the ten-legged bear and then fled to an iceberg that was split by a narrow fissure. He ran into the crack and out the other side. The bear followed, but became stuck in the crack. Safe from Kuqqugiaq's fifty talons, the man stabbed the bear to death with his spear.

Winter itself, suggested the Chukchi people of Eastern Siberia, was a dreadful frost giant that descended from the north and lay in sleep across the face of their land. People and animals alike were forced by his snowy presence to hide or flee. The polar bears, though, could move about. And when a mother bear gave birth to a mischievous cub, it crawled into the frost giant's nose and made him sneeze. Awake, the frost giant became lonesome for his family and returned to his home in the distant north, allowing summer's warmth to prevail.

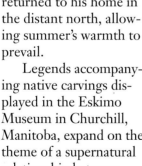

Legends accompanying native carvings displayed in the Eskimo Museum in Churchill, Manitoba, expand on the theme of a supernatural relationship between polar bears and people:

"A man waiting at a seal hole was surprised by a bear," relates one account. "The man's two dogs attacked the bear, allowing the man to kill the bear with his knife. At death the bear turned into the man's mother-in-law. She had assumed the form of a bear to frighten him. He killed the bear not knowing it was his mother-in-law."

Of a display of tiny prehistoric carvings in bone, the museum caption states:

"It has been suggested that many of the animal carvings of bears represent the spirit helpers of the shaman, helping spirits embodied in the animal carvings which the shaman dangled from his belt or outer clothing parts or in special bags or containers. The bear may have been part of a shaman's magical equipment to help him embark on 'spirit flights' to visit the spirits, in order to consult with them, to

seek information about offenses against them or their taboos, to appease them, or to invoke their help to overcome adverse conditions."

In all the frozen world, there was nothing that so stirred an Eskimo hunter's blood as much as the sight of a polar bear. Writing of his turn-of-the-century life as a priest with Canada's Coppermine Eskimos, Roger P. Buliard observed in his book *Inuk* that:

"An Eskimo may catch a thousand fish, and never a word of boasting will be heard, but let him kill a bear and then the news will travel, far and fast. 'Nanuktorok,' the Inuit will say of the fortunate hunter. 'He has killed a bear.'

"For in the Arctic, the bear is the champion, the greatest prize.

"The polar bear enjoys legendary status among all northern peoples. 'He is God's dog,' whisper the Lapps, who call Nanuk 'the old man in the fur cloak,' afraid to use his proper name for fear he will overhear them and be offended.

"'He has twelve men's strength and eleven men's wit,' sang the Norsemen of the sagas. The Norse poets called him 'the white sea deer,' 'the whale's bane,' 'the seal's dread,' 'the rider of icebergs,' and 'the sailor of the floe.'"

But until European explorers introduced the firearm, Eskimos lacked the means to take polar bears in numbers that endangered survival of the species. For those possessed of bullets and gunpowder, it was too easy.

In his book *A Voyage Towards the North Pole*, published in 1803, the British naval officer C. J. Phipps described an encounter with a mother bear and her two cubs that was typical for the day. She had been drawn to the side of the ship by the smell of a butchered "sea horse" (or walrus) that had been killed earlier.

"The crew of the ship . . . threw out great lumps of the flesh . . . , which the old bear fetched away . . . and laid each clump before her cubs as she brought it, and dividing it, gave each a share, reserving a small portion for herself. As she was fetching away the last piece . . . , the crew leveled their muskets at the cubs and shot them both dead. They also wounded the dam, but not mortally. . . . Though she was sorely wounded, and could but just crawl to the place where they lay, she carried the lump of flesh that they had fetched away . . . and laid it down before them. When she saw that they refused to eat, she laid her paws first on one and then upon the other and endeavored to raise them up. All this while she made the most pitiful moans, and when she found that she could not stir them . . . she began to lick their wounds. . . . Finding at last that they were cold and lifeless, she raised her head toward the ship and seemed to growl a curse upon the murderers, which they returned with a volley of musket balls. She fell between her cubs and died licking their wounds."

A hundred years later, a few men in the North had learned a measure of respect for the courage and fidelity of a mother polar bear. Writing in 1925 in *Plain Tales of the Far North*, Capt. Thierry Mallet described a day when his steamship came upon a mother and her two cubs on pack ice near Baffin Island. Armed with rifles, the skipper and crew began to chase the trio through the pack ice in the steamship. When the cubs were too exhausted to continue:

"The mother and cubs scrambled on to a piece of ice a few yards in front of the steamer. . . . The little cubs were done. They just lay on the ice and panted. The mother could have taken to the water . . . but she remained beside her young, facing the ship squarely, silently, fearlessly. Her jaws were half

With its big body and its small ears and tail, a polar bear is a classic example of Bergmann's rule, which suggests that colder temperatures encourage the survival of larger animals.

open in a snarl. Now and then she would lift a front paw and cuff the air as if she wanted to show how hard she could hit our steel stem if ever our vessel touched her.

"There was a silence on board. Suddenly our skipper's voice rang out: 'Hard over at port,' while the telegraph rang. 'Full speed ahead.' The same voice called out again, 'Leave those bears alone, you sons of bitches.'

"As the ship swung over—gathered way and passed the pan of ice—three blasts of the steamer's foghorn blared out in a salute! It was the old Newfoundland master. He was leaning over the side of his bridge, waving to the old she-bear who still stood, undaunted, right over the bodies of her two little cubs."

Along with growing knowledge of polar bears and their life cycle has come greater respect and admiration for a truly remarkable animal. And of all the subpopulations, that of Canada's Churchill Wildlife Management Area is best known. Some 1,500 animals occupy this range that encompasses the western shore of Hudson Bay and centers on the historic town of Churchill, founded in 1717.

For centuries, humans have lived compatibly with polar bears here. After 1930, when railroad connections were completed to the newly constructed port of Churchill, scientists began to visit the town to study its wildlife. During the 1970s, the community gained a measure of notoriety as a place where polar bears wandered in the streets and feasted on garbage at the town dump. Curiosity seekers began to visit Churchill to see the bears. Today they find that the dump has been cleaned up and bears are hard to find.

On the cape, however, there are bears for all to see. Moments after we park along the esker's icy shore, Nanuk arrives to keep us company. Another soon ambles over to see what we are up to. Numbers three and four follow. By the end of the day, we have 20 polar bears of various ages and sexes lolling about our vehicle. As many as 60 bears have been observed together here in years past.

Despite the observation of Danish explorer Peter Freuchen that polar bears are "the loneliest creatures on earth," these seem to like each other's company.

Left: A mother bear challenges an approaching male, to protect her cub-of-the-year. The male backs away, but not far enough to satisfy the female, who follows with her cub.

Russia's leading polar bear zoologist, Dr. Nikita Ovsianikov, explains that just because bears often travel alone over ice doesn't mean that they are anti-social. "They make friends," he says. "They tolerate each other in close contact. They are happy to be surrounded by other bears. Adult males, particularly, have well developed friendships."

One of our young males strolls over to an older male and invites him to play-fight. The challenger rises to his hind legs, letting his front paws hang down by his side. He lowers his chin to his chest and by his posture says, "Let's play." His chosen partner stands, and they grapple like a pair of sumo wrestlers idly practicing their skills. They push and pull, twist and turn, scuffle in the snow, mouth each other, and slap with their paws. But they are careful to pull their punches. The bears mimic battles they may one day fight over a female. For now, it's all in fun. The two dance a ponderous waltz until one pushes the other down. They roll in the snow, pawing lazily at each other. After half an hour, they get bored with it and go to sleep in each other's arms. An hour later, they are at it again.

Along with the other spectators, a mother and COY, or "cub-of-the-year," arrive at our camp. Females usually have two cubs, although one or three or even four cubs may be born. When this mother emerged from her birth den south of the cape, she probably introduced a set of twins to their world of snow and ice. But between March and November she's very likely lost one to wolves or adult male polar bears or accidental injury. Six out of 10 cubs born die during their first year, researchers report.

With one cub remaining, the mother is doubly cautious about the safety of her child. When one of the jolly wrestlers nearby wakes up and wanders near, she tells him to take his short, furry tail elsewhere. She speaks to her cub with low huffing grunts, ordering him to get behind her and stay there. Quickly, he stations himself at her heels. With baby in tow, mother advances on the offensive male, who is fully three times her size. She assumes a hostile posture with head down and upper lip curled. He turns his head aside in a peacemaking gesture. She will have none of it. Lunging with jaws agape, she tries for a bite on his neck or ears. He scuttles away, fending her off with open muzzle. Again she charges and he retreats. Behind his mother, baby imitates her every move with open mouth and tenor growls. Feinting with her open jaws, the female rushes at the male yet again, and when he parries, she delivers a powerful left hook to his side. The blow knocks him off his feet. Flat on his back, great legs flailing, he rolls in the flying snow before scrambling again to his feet. The relentless termagant presses her attack and the male surrenders. The picture of injured innocence, he turns and strolls off to a snowdrift perhaps a hundred yards away. Here, he scrapes out a day bed and curls up in it, leaving the ill-tempered hussy to go about her business.

The male, big-boned, heavily muscled, and three times as large as the 350-pound female, could very likely have killed her had he chosen to do so. But he would certainly have suffered severe injury in the fight. Instinctively, he knows that in the Arctic, an injured animal is a dead animal. For polar bears, symbolic confrontation is sufficient in a land where the struggle to maintain life itself is an epic battle on a daily basis.

One enthralled polar bear watcher, peering out the window as the struggle between the mother and the intruder is concluded, accidentally dislodges his karakul hat. It falls out of the window and 10 feet to the ice below. Instantly, two mischievous subadults, young four-year-old males, pounce on the fur with obvious glee. One seizes it and scampers away with the other pursuing. A game of arctic keep-away surges back and forth on the ice for nearly an hour. Finally, the two overgrown cubs tear the hat to shreds and eat it. "What'll I tell my wife?" the hat-less observer wonders. "She'll never believe that polar bears ate it."

Having disposed of the hat, the two juveniles try a new game. One dives into shallow water near the edge of some slushy new ice. Swimming underneath, he breaks through with his head and pops up like a surfacing seal near his friend. The second teenager rushes to grab his pal, who promptly submerges. It's ursine tag, with one bear playing the role of seal and the other trying to catch him. Finally, the bear in the water loses interest and crawls out. Not realizing the game is over, the "it" bear crouches at the hole for half an hour, waiting for his friend to reappear.

His playmate, however, is drying his fur in the snow. It's an important bit of hygiene, for fur that is dirty or wet is a poor insulator. Dry snow will absorb the water from his pelage. The bear places his chin and chest on a patch of clean snow and with his bottom high in the air, plows through the drift by pushing with his hind feet. The front done, he splays his hind legs and sits, pulling his rear end through the snow with his front paws. Rolling onto his back, he squirms and wriggles, great feet waving in the air. Then each side gets its turn. Scooping up snow with his paws, he uses it as a towel for his face. A thorough, careful job restores his pelage.

Dry again, the bear saunters over to our parked vehicle to satisfy his curiosity. He walks around it,

sniffing the tires and eyeing the occupants. He appears to decide that it would be nice to join us. Finding no way in, he stands and places his paws against the side of the open photography platform and gives it a shove. This movement is the same used by bears to break into the subnivean lairs of mother seals. When a bear pushes, things move. The six-ton vehicle rocks and shakes. He finds this quite satisfying, and pushes again. After several small earthquakes Len Smith, wise in the ways of bears, goes out onto the platform. He doubles up his formidable fist and smacks the bear on his sensitive nose. Blinking in surprise, the bear backs away, and sits down to consider this development.

Shortly, the vehicle shakes again as the persistent bear takes up where he left off. Irked, Smith returns to the platform, makes a fist, and swings again at the bear's nose. This time, the bear ducks. Smith's punch goes wide. Having made his point, the bear goes off for a nap.

Has Len Smith risked injury by taking a poke at a bear? No. Smith, who has 20 years of experience dealing with bears, was using standard procedure for discouraging them, albeit not one recommended for beginners. (A length of broomstick serves as well.) He knows that polar bears are not normally given to violent aggression. With no interest in defending territory, polar bears have no reason to be the raging aggressors of popular myth.

For example, a popular American television documentary film records a sequence in which a polar bear appears to attack a man protected by a steel cage. The filming took place a few yards from where our vehicle now stands.

But awed viewers don't get to see what really happened. The intrepid adventurer couldn't get the bears to perform for his cameras. When he sat in the cage, the bears ignored a script calling for them to attack him. While the "bait" fretted, the bears dozed. Finally, in desperation, the adventurer smeared the cage with sardines. Attracted by the tasty fish, a bear wandered over and began licking them from the bars. In his enthusiasm, the bear pushed over the cage. The daredevil inside pretended to be in fear of his life.

He was not in mortal danger, as Dr. Nikita Ovsianikov has shown in the course of researching the behavior of polar bears on Wrangel Island. Ovsianikov walks routinely among bears that visit Wrangel to prey on walrus females and calves that congregate there in summer. When approached by a bear, Ovsianikov uses the vocalization and posture that bears employ themselves to warn away other bears. "I stand up and step toward the bear belligerently," he says. "I look at him fiercely, and I hiss at him. This tells the bear that I am dominant where I am, and that he is not to intrude in my territory. He will respect that. He'll go away and keep his distance."

Ovsianikov explains that polar bears are normally cautious in confrontations, fighting only when provoked and preferring retreat and escape.

It is this kind of information that scientists of the five polar bear nations are patiently assembling through far-ranging research. Biologists of both Canada and the United States pursue ongoing programs in which individual animals are tranquilized for study. Some are outfitted with radio telemetry collars that permit their movements to be followed via satellite.

"Polar bears are not easily studied," observes Dr. Gerald Garner, who supervises polar bear research in Alaska for the United States Fish and Wildlife Service. "We can't follow them around. Yet we need

to develop accurate census data and get more reliable population estimates. Also, we must learn more about the movement of bears within a given range. We have no idea of where they go during the year and why they go there."

Sensible conservation policies require reliable data, Garner points out. "We don't enjoy tranquilizing bears, but it is our only option."

Pursued by biologists in helicopters, polar bears understandably believe themselves to be under attack. When escape fails, they will defend themselves bravely. Steve Miller's helicopter has been charged many times over the past 10 years in the course of a research program in which scientists with the Canadian Parks Service have successfully and safely darted and tranquilized more than 2,300 bears.

The most experienced of the world's helicopter pilots in low-level arctic flying, Miller drops to within 20 feet of a bear so that a scientist marksman won't miss when shooting it with a hypodermic dart full of a tranquilizing drug. Once the bear goes to sleep, usually a matter of several minutes, Miller lands the chopper beside it and biologists emerge to weigh the animal, determine its age and sex, and appraise its overall health. If it hasn't been tagged with a numbered ear button, they plug one in. They stand guard over the bear until it wakes up, then leave to find another.

Usually, that's how it goes, Miller says. But mothers protecting cubs often turn and try to drive off the hovering threat. "They'll jump at the helicopter and swat at it," he says. "And if that doesn't work, they will hide their cubs under their bodies and defy us."

On one such occasion, a tranquilizing mishap almost cost a mother bear her life.

"She was in shallow water near the landfast ice," Miller says. "When we approached, she shooed her cubs onto the ice and was following them when the dart struck." Normally, the bear would have had plenty of time to get out of the water and onto the ice. But this time, the dart pierced an artery and the drug took effect instantly.

"She sagged and sank," Miller recalls.

Without hesitation, the two Canadian scientists leaped out of the helicopter into the icy sea water. They held up the mother's head so she could breathe, and with frantic effort, hauled her onto the ice. In danger themselves of death from hypothermia, the two men stripped and dried their bodies while the mother snored beside them.

"The natives shoot and kill bears all the time," Miller says, "but we didn't want one to die on our account."

Not all visitors to the area become so involved with polar bears. Each fall, 3,000 venturers arrive at Churchill, the polar bear viewing capital of the world, in the hope of seeing the prototypical animal of the Far North. Chances for a sighting are best during October and the first two weeks of November, when the bears concentrate along the bay shore.

Each day, buses take groups out to Launch Point a few miles east of Churchill in search of bears. They usually succeed. For those joining the Cape Churchill safari, bears close-up and personal are a virtual certainty, as are the comfort and safety of the observers.

Once winter closes in, with temperatures down to 40 degrees below zero and nights 20 hours long, polar bear viewing becomes too difficult and dangerous for all but native hunters.

As spring approaches, mother bears bring their newly born cubs out of their birth dens in late March and early April. But observing, much less photographing, this event is beyond the resources of most people. In many parts of the High Arctic, females den on the sea ice itself. Denning areas are also found on hillside slopes near the sea. All are exceedingly remote and difficult to find. In addition, females with newborn cubs are extremely wary and will not emerge if they sense the presence of a human being.

Late spring viewing is possible by boat in Wager Bay, where a 93-mile rift notches the northwestern shore of Hudson Bay. Bears gather there to feed on seals that congregate on Wager Bay's ice pack in large numbers.

Seeing polar bears on Alaskan ice presents difficulties too great for any but the most dedicated of wildlife watchers. There are good reasons why three out of four Alaskan Eskimos have never seen a wild polar bear. Aside from hiring a helicopter and crisscrossing the pack ice of the Bering or the Beaufort seas, the polar bear viewer must hire a guide, go out on the ice with a dog team, and camp there, often for weeks, before being rewarded by the sight of one, perhaps two bears.

What follows is distilled from years of polar bear watching.

Facing page: A strange bear approaching a mother and her two COYs leads mom to assume a protective stance; one of her cubs, probably a male because he is larger, stands to get a better look.

Mothers and Cubs

Facing page: When mom settled down for a nap, her male cub grabbed the warmest spot on his mother's backside, while his sister had to be satisfied with last place.

Motherhood for female polar bears usually begins when the female reaches sexual maturity around the age of four years. She comes into estrus in spring, an event noted by every mature male in her vicinity. The sole parental role of male polar bears is to impregnate females, and they fight fiercely among themselves over the right to copulate with her. The winner, usually the largest and most determined of the suitors, proceeds to mate with the female repeatedly. Once this is done, the male goes back to the hunt, his responsibility as a father ended.

After she is impregnated, usually in April or early May, the female's body will delay implantation of the fertilized eggs throughout the summer. Her uterus is capable of holding several of them in abeyance until the time comes to begin gestation.

In anticipation of the demands of gestation, the female will eat heavily, seeking to double or even triple her weight. In late August or early September, implantation takes place. If her fat reserves are satisfactory, the usual two embryos will implant. If she has had an exceptionally good year, she might go for three or even four babies. But if she is thin and in poor health, her body may limit pregnancy to one embryo, or even absorb all of them in favor of conserving her limited resources.

With babies on the way, she needs a suitable birth den. Females in the High Arctic and off the North Slope of Alaska may choose to dig a cave in a snowdrift accumulated in the lee of a pressure ridge in old pack ice. Bears in the Churchill Wildlife Management Area den along the banks of the Broad River or the Owl River south of the cape. The most favored den sites are to be found on the slopes of mountains or hills near the sea. On Wrangel Island, which lies off the eastern Siberian coast in the Chukchi Sea, some 500 den sites have been mapped on hillsides near the seashore. Whether a mother returns to the site of her own birth, scientists can't say for sure. Dr. Nikita Ovsianikov, Russia's leading polar bear zoologist, says he lacks firm proof, but he believes females do

Right: At 10 months, this cub hadn't yet learned how to sit on clear ice without losing his footing.

Preceding pages: Ice floes, where seals haul out to rest, are the end of the rainbow for hungry polar bears.

come back to the area where they were born to make their own birth dens and give birth to their own cubs.

Having chosen her spot, the female tunnels into the deep snow and fashions two chambers connected by a passageway. The usual den has an oval upper chamber, perhaps four feet in height and five feet wide, and a smaller chamber downslope, which is vented to admit air. Using her claws, she models and smooths the den's interior, removing enough snow from the roof to admit air and a little light.

The cubs are born in November or December. At birth they are fully furred, about 12 to 14 inches long, and they weigh a little more than a pound. Nursing on their mother's rich milk, which to human taste is strong and rank, the cubs grow rapidly. Their mother covers their small feces and urine stains with snow to keep the den clean and almost odorless. Within two months, cubs are able to move about inside the den. By late March or early April, the cubs will have reached the size of a Sealyham terrier and will weigh around 16 pounds.

In early spring, the cubs make their debut. Their mother breaks through the concealing snow, sticks out her head, and takes a look around. If it isn't too cold, and no predators appear, she will enlarge the den opening and come outside. She will lift her head and sniff the air. If she detects an unusual scent, she will go back into the den and stay there until the following day. But if all seems safe, she will call her cubs to her with a low breathy grunt. The babies emerge cautiously and awkwardly, with muscles and skills as yet undeveloped. For several days, she will let them play outside the den and grow accustomed to their new world.

At this time, the mother needs food. Though not hibernating she hasn't eaten since the previous August or September and has been converting her body's fat reserves into protein for both herself and her cubs. Her compelling need is to reactivate her digestive system. Scraping away the snow cover on slopes near the den, she grazes on grass and sedge until she can produce a bowel movement. Then, with the kids in tow, she heads for the pack ice, where she can resume feeding on seals.

A cub that is less than a year old is called a cub-of-the-year, or COY, regardless of how many cubs there were in the litter.

COYs learn early to eat the red meat their mother catches for them, while she consumes the seal's blubber. Until they are sufficiently large and experienced to catch and defend their own kills,

Facing page: When a strange bear approaches, all three members of this family take note of the intruder's appearance and scent. Youngsters are taught to stay near their mother and get behind her if danger threatens.

Below: Three months old and weighing about 16 pounds, this COY is being taken by his mother from his birth den to the sea ice of Hudson Bay, where she will catch seals for them to eat.

cubs make do with leftovers. They continue to nurse for more than a year while practicing to be polar bears.

By the time they are two years old, yearlings will be almost as big as their mother and able to fend for themselves. At that time, mothers in the Low Arctic will drive away or abandon the youngsters and prepare to mate once again. Because they mate more often, mothers in the Low Arctic may have up to 10

litters. In the High Arctic, where food is less plentiful, cubs remain with their mother an additional year. Thus a female will produce a litter of cubs only once every two to four years. Over the course of her reproductive life, a wild polar bear female will have no more than five to eight litters, which may represent a total of no more than ten to fifteen cubs.

On average, six of ten cubs will not survive their first year of life. Starvation, accident, and predation (including killing of the cubs or their mothers by Eskimo hunters) take a heavy toll of COYs. Adult male polar bears will kill cubs, as well, if they can catch them.

The near-half of each year's crop of cubs that lives through the first year of life is testimony to the fierceness with which their mothers protect them and the attentive nurturing they receive. Like mothers of all species, young and inexperienced polar bear mothers make mistakes. But once she gets the hang of it, a polar bear mother is a model parent. Affectionate and devoted, she is tolerant of her babies' needs but strict in her regulation of their behavior. Nowhere in nature is there a better example of dedicated motherhood.

Right: A yearling cub, in front, and his mother, in back, make a formidable pair in battling others for possession of food. The youngster will continue to pretend his mother is near even after he is on his own.

Left: The two larger cubs in this litter of three have bloodied the ear of their smaller sister, whose chances of living out the year are small.

Facing page: At 10 months old, this cub-of-the-year has a good start on life. He is probably the surviving cub of twins.

Left: Polar bear females are good mothers and give their cubs lots of love and kisses. She licks them clean and makes sure they stay warm and dry.

Right: While mother rests on a frozen tidal pond, her two cubs take shelter from the wind. They have not yet acquired the thick layer of blubber that protects her from the chill.

Below: Told to stay behind his mother, a COY waits for her to decide what to do about an approaching stranger.

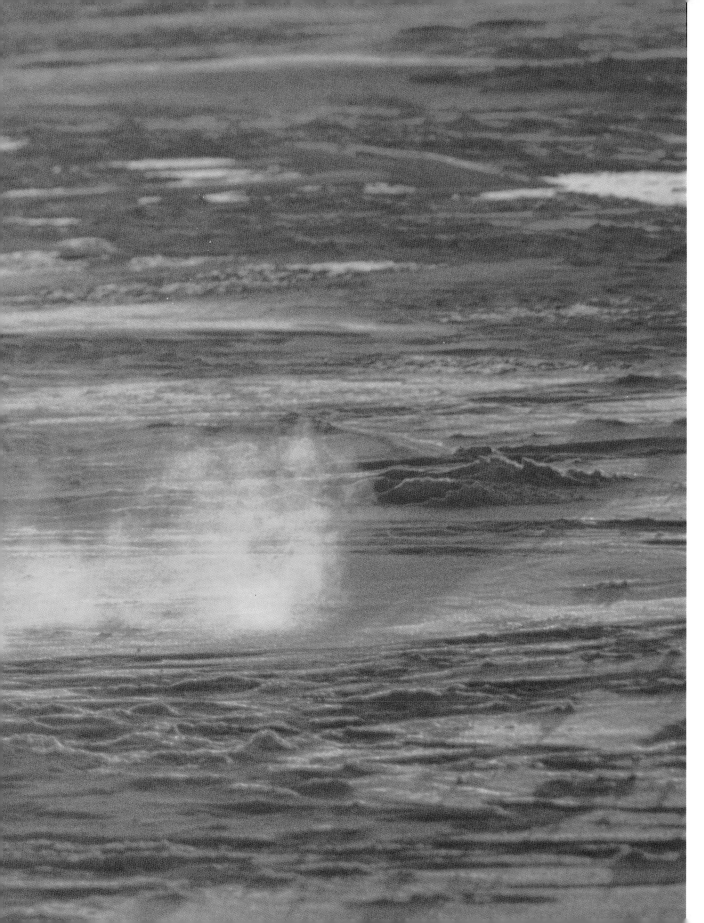

This mother bear is breathing hard because she has just chased away a large adult male who threatened her cub.

Left: Another bear, approaching a mother and her two COYs, is still far enough away to cause her no concern.

Below and right: When the intruder comes too close, the mother warns him away while the two cubs stand to watch how she does it.

Left: Like all bears, polar bears are capable of standing erect, even as cubs, and often do so to watch other bears.

Right: This family, consisting of a female and two yearling cubs, has just come ashore after taking a swim. They are grooming themselves by rolling in the snow.

Left: Although he has made it through first eight months of life, this cub has a lot to learn if he is to survive. More than half of all cubs die within a year of birth.

Below: When this yearling cub's mother catches a seal, she will eat the fat and he the lean protein that he needs for growth.

On the Move

P olar bears are not especially swift, although they can dash as fast as a horse for a short distance. They are not particularly agile, although they are quick enough to catch and kill a wriggling seal. But they are Arctic Argonauts, wandering hundreds of miles over broken sea ice and swimming equal distances through frigid seas. Nothing in nature excels the polar bear. They may be found anywhere within the eight million square miles circumscribed by the 50° F isotherm line for July that serves as one of the preferred boundaries of the Arctic region.

Comdr. James Calvert, writing in 1966 about the voyage of the atomic submarine *Skate* under the permanent polar ice pack of the Arctic Ocean to the North Pole, recalled a day in August when he brought the boat up through the ice to the surface.

"There was nothing but a flat patchwork maze of ice floes in every direction," he wrote, except that "slowly climbing out of the water and up onto the ice was a full-grown polar bear. He shook himself like a wet dog and gazed curiously at this intruder in his domain."

For prowling snow and ice, no animal is more appropriately equipped.

A polar bear's foot is almost as broad as it is wide, and in a mature adult male, can be 12 inches long. Hair fringes the sides and extends between the toes, but the pads are bare. They are covered with what some scientists have suggested are tiny suction cups that provide traction on ice. The toes are slightly webbed, an advantage in swimming. The black claws are slender, hooked, sharp, and flexible. Their design heightens the bear's grip on ice and makes a superior tool for snaring an escaping seal. A polar bear can pick up an object using its claws like fishhooks.

The polar bear's front feet turn inward slightly, giving it a pigeon-toed walk and perhaps a slight advantage in slapping or grasping prey.

With its slender Roman nose, long powerful neck, relatively short forelegs, and massive hindquarters, the polar bear constitutes a living derrick designed to yank a large seal

through a small breathing hole, crushing its bones, and onto the ice where it can be eaten.

While a polar bear can walk for hours at a brisk pace, he prefers not to hurry. He likes a leisurely stroll. Plodding across pack ice, swinging his head back and forth, lifting his nose occasionally to sniff the air, a bear watches where he is going and puts his feet down with care. He avoids bare ice and will go out of his way to walk on snow, which provides better traction. His wide flat paws exert less pressure per square inch on the ice than do the feet of a man. He can walk over ice too thin to hold up a man. Crossing rubbery new ice, a bear will reduce the impact of his weight still further by lying on his stomach and spreading his legs. He slides, pulling with his front claws.

A straight-line animal, he prefers to go over rather than around an obstacle. His tracks in the snow as he crosses an ice field rarely deviate. A polar bear attracted by an interesting sight or odor, will turn at a precise angle and head for it.

Marathon swimmers, polar bears have been found paddling along in the open ocean miles from

land. "In 1908," wrote Capt. Thierry Mallet in his book *Plain Tales of the North*, "we saw a white bear yearling cub swimming towards shore at least fifteen miles out from Cape Churchill in Hudson Bay. The nearest ice was then forty-five miles from the spot where we found him. There was absolutely no doubt that our bear had undertaken a sixty-mile swim to reach land." Elsewhere, scientists logged one nonstop swim by a polar bear of 200 miles.

COYs sometimes ride on their mother's back when she swims or when she walks in deep snow. Adult bears routinely get around on ice floes, as well, often riding their icy rafts for long distances. In recent times, one animal was borne from the Bering Strait 500 miles south to the Pribilof Islands, where it went ashore and was killed by frightened Aleuts. The bears of the Cape Churchill area routinely ride ice floes to land in the spring when break-up occurs in Hudson Bay. A polar bear tagged at Svalbard, a Norwegian island in the Arctic Ocean halfway between Norway and Greenland, was found 18 months later in southern Greenland after covering a distance of 2,000 miles.

Left: A mother with two yearling cubs leads the way across pack ice in Wager Bay, in the Canadian Subarctic.

Left: A mother bear climbs onto an ice floe, followed closely by her son and daughter.

Facing page: A mother bear waits for her smaller, slower daughter to catch up.

Left: A polar bear spreads his legs to stay on top of thin ice.

Below: Slushy ice beginning to solidify in November's deepening cold proves too thin for a polar bear's weight and his left rear paw breaks through.

"He can walk over ice too thin to hold up a man. Crossing rubbery new ice, a bear will reduce the impact of his weight still further by lying on his stomach and spreading his legs. He slides, pulling with his front claws."

Left and above: A polar bear must spread his legs wide to walk on this ice. He makes it almost to the shoreline before the rotten ice gives way underneath his hindquarters.

Polar bears communicate through scent, body posture, physical action that involves touching noses or mouthing, and by calls that include low moans, snorts, explosive hisses, and when angry, loud growls and roars.

A polar bear's roman nose, long neck, relatively short front legs and massive hindquarters help him catch the seals on which he lives.

From a Wrangel Island hill-top, a polynya, or lead of open water, in the Chukchi Sea gives seals a place to haul out and polar bears a place to hunt.

Two adult males play a game of tag with one popping up through a hole in the ice, the other trying to catch him.

"They are Arctic Argonauts, wandering hundreds of miles over broken sea ice and swimming equal distances through frigid seas; nothing in nature excels the polar bear"

Left: In summer, polar bears may often be found on the rocky shores of islands and peninsulas near the ocean.

Below: Polar bears regularly groom their paws to remove ice that cakes between their toes. They may find an accumulation of ice to be uncomfortable when walking or it may affect their traction on slippery surfaces.

Endless Days, Endless Nights

The sterile ice of the arctic environment seems a poor place to make a living. But for polar bears, the ocean beneath the frozen surface furnishes food aplenty. Millions of ringed, bearded, and harp seals live here, attracted by rich schools of fish and the bottom-dwelling relatives of crab and shrimp found in warmer waters. When seals haul out on the ice to rest, or when they surface in breathing holes for a breath of air, polar bears are waiting.

Bears use their superb sense of smell to find breathing holes in the ice beneath a carpet of snow. A seal usually makes several holes, and a hunting bear cannot know which one the seal will use. But the bear knows to settle down and wait beside one hole, rarely waiting more than an hour for the seal to come.

At the hole, the bear crouches, olfactory senses alert. As the slightest movement will cause the snow to crunch or squeak, the bear must remain perfectly still so as not to alert the seal below. When the seal surfaces, it exhales. Smelling the fishy breath, the bear instantly shoves a paw into the hole and hooks the seal, biting the seal's head to crush its skull and quickly dragging the carcass away from the hole.

When seals haul out on the edge of the ice

near a lead of open water, they know they are at risk. Every three or four minutes, a resting seal raises its head and looks around for danger. Seeing none, it lowers its head and naps briefly. A hungry bear, seeing the seal, walks toward it to within a hundred yards, then crouches. When the seal isn't looking, the bear creeps closer. If the bear succeeds in approaching to within 30 to 40 feet of the seal, it attacks in a sudden, furious rush. Sometimes the bear catches the seal, but as often as not, the seal escapes to safety in the water nearby.

In several of his books about his adventures in the Arctic, explorer Peter Freuchen mentions a popular belief that a stalking polar bear will cover its black nose with its white paw so as to conceal it from a resting seal. Yet, of all the zoologists who have spent thousands of hours watching polar bears hunt, not one has ever seen a hunting bear do this. They believe it to be one more myth among the many told about polar bears.

A bear that has made a kill feeds immediately, knowing that other bears will smell the blood and seek a share. A mature bear will eat the skin and blubber for the calories contained, and leaving the red meat, wander off. Young bears, who need the protein, will make a meal of the remaining carrion, while arctic foxes and gulls will clean up what's left. Seal bones found on the ice are invariably picked clean.

Bears get annoyed at the arctic foxes that follow at their heels, and sometimes charge them. The tiny foxes are ordinarily too fast and agile to fall prey to a slow, clumsy bear. But foxes make mistakes. For instance, I've seen a fox become preoccupied with a scrap of food. A bear pretended to walk by, then suddenly whirled and swatted the fox with a powerful paw. The blow broke the little animal's back. The bear ripped open the carcass and licked the intestines briefly before losing interest and walking away. The arctic fox, which weighs only about seven

pounds, offers nothing to an animal capable of eating 140 pounds of meat in one meal. On another occasion, an eider duck walked near a snoozing bear that was hidden by a blanket of snow. The bear awoke, saw the eider, and lunged. The duck managed to get about three feet off the ground before the bear's jaws clamped shut on it. Again, the bear did little more than sniff at the carcass before going back to sleep.

Sometimes the fox outsmarts the bear. Some years ago, crewmen on board a rig drilling for oil in the Beaufort Sea, near Banks Island, watched as an arctic fox tricked a mother bear and stole a meal.

The polar bear, a female with a COY, had killed a seal at a lead in the ice just 100 feet from the rig. She ate the blubber, then brought her baby to the carcass so that it could eat some of the red meat. But the cub wanted to nurse and refused to eat. Nearby, several arctic foxes waited impatiently to share the kill. Each time a fox approached the meat, the mother would drive it away.

At this point, a large male fox began trotting in a circle around the bear and her cub. By approaching closely on the side away from the kill, the fox teased the polar bear into charging, and drew her farther and farther away from the meat. The cub followed at its mother's heels. When she had left the carcass exposed, one of the other foxes rushed in to grab a bite. The mother dashed back to protect her kill, leaving her infant. Instantly, the male fox sprang at the cub and nipped it on the flank. The cub squealed, and the mother bear raced back to protect her child. Without missing a step, the male fox closed on the carcass, grabbed it and ran off with the others following close behind. The mother bear, inspecting her cub for injury, could only watch.

Facing page: Polar bears that have not matured sexually are called subadults. Females mature at four or five years, males at five or six years.

Left: Cleaning his back in the snow, a polar bear displays the pads of his feet, black like his skin and tongue, which are pitted with tiny cups that give added traction on icy surfaces.

Facing page: With his long muzzle and neck, a polar bear is well suited for searching out seals in their breathing holes. Except for the carrion of a beached whale or walrus and a small amount of kelp or grass found along a shoreline, polar bears rely almost entirely on seals as food.

"Bears use their superb sense of smell to find breathing holes in the ice beneath a carpet of snow. A seal usually makes several holes, and a hunting bear cannot know which one the seal will use. But the bear knows to settle down and wait beside one hole, rarely waiting more than an hour for the seal to come."

Right: Having surprised and killed a ringed seal, an adult polar bear eats the skin and blubber, leaving the red meat.

Arctic foxes commonly follow adult polar bears and consume the red meat that the bear does not normally eat.

Too old and slow to catch a speedy arctic fox, an adult male polar bear plays 'possum,' then lunges when the fox strays near, though not near enough.

A year-round resident of the arctic regions, the arctic fox preys upon lemmings and ptarmigan, supplemented with carrion from polar bear kills.

Right: Exposed to severe subzero cold, a polar bear increases fat metabolism so as to maintain body heat at a comfortable temperature.

Preceding pages: Left, grooming is important to health and comfort among polar bears. After waking from a nap, a bear scrubs his back in a drift of dry snow. Right, this young female, approaching the age of three years, will mate in another year or two and will have from five to eight litters of cubs in her lifetime.

Polar bears are so well insulated that they give off no
detectable heat. Their body temperature, at rest, is the same
as that of humans: 98.6° F.

While polar bears do not hibernate, as do black and brown bears,
they enjoy frequent naps, especially during the heat of summer.
They continue to hunt and move about throughout the year.

Right: The face of this large adult male reveals the scars that a lifetime of mating battles have inflicted.

Below: A polar bear's pigeon-toed front paws are an asset in grasping and gripping prey.

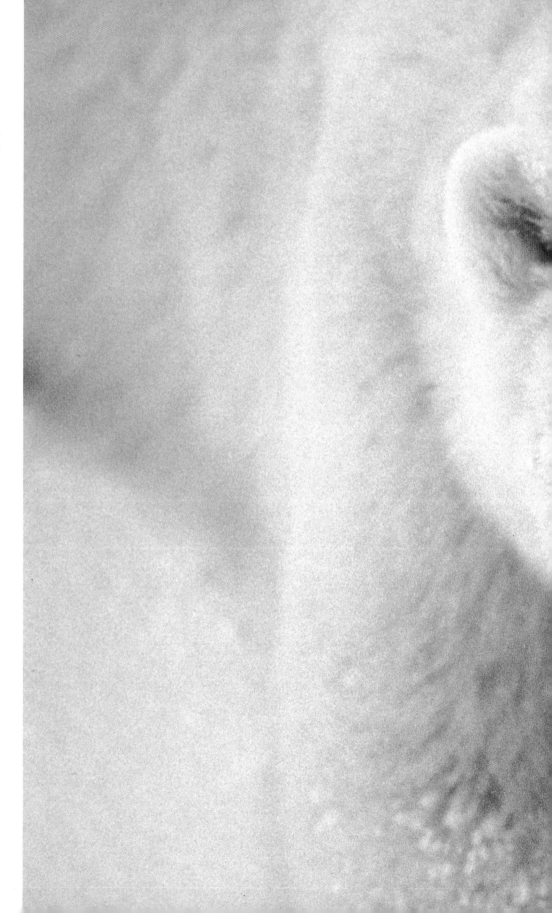

Skirting the land-fast ice on the rocks of a Wager Bay shoreline, a hungry male polar bear watches for seals that might haul out where the ice and open water meet.

Playing Together

Facing page: If they don't know each other, bears will circle and sniff each other's scent to become aquainted.

Right: After vigorous play, a time-out and rest period may ensue.

Preceding pages: The Arctic is actually a desert receiving no more than two to five inches of moisture a year, mostly in the form of snow.

To most people, polar bears seem like vicious and ferocious beasts that may be approached only with caution and proper safeguards. And perhaps that's the wisest way to deal with any wild animal, whether carnivorous or herbivorous. Even so, it is hard to maintain a sense of fear in the presence of a creature as playful and seemingly friendly as a polar bear.

High on a Wrangel Island slope, for example, I saw three cubs at play, their mother watching over them. One sat on his haunches and careened downhill like a small toboggan. Scampering back to the top, he slid down again. With his mother watching benignly, he slid down a third time and a fourth. While scientists caution against assigning human emotions to wild animals, even the most objective of observers would find it difficult to interpret the cub's gleeful look and big grin as anything other than pleasure. His siblings, meanwhile, were taking turns leaping onto each other and rolling over and over in the snow. Of course the little bears were exercising their muscles and developing their reflexes, but like human children, they were having loads of fun doing it.

Adult bears, especially the most youthful males among them, play as well. Zoologists call it play-fighting, and suggest that their games constitute a friendly means of practicing the physical skills a sexually active adult bear needs to compete successfully in the springtime mating wars. Older adult males seem less inclined to play. Possibly they already possess fighting skills, or maybe they are just tired. Yet an older bear may seemingly accept the role of teacher or coach of a younger male. Young females may sometimes play with a male sibling, but never with other males. Conceivably they have no need of play-fighting skills.

One particularly long session of play began at Cape Churchill on November 17, 1991, at 10 o'clock in the morning, with the temperature at 32.6° F. It was to last for four days.

Two of the bears were handsome 5-year-olds, each weighing perhaps 600 pounds. Sleek, fat, and mischievous, they were the ursine incarnation of Hans and Fritz, the Katzenjammer Kids. Their older friend was a scuffed and scarred 11-year-old male of 1,000 pounds or more. Patches of black hide showed through his white pelage where divots of hair had been removed by the claws and teeth of other bears, probably in fights over a female. The name of Bruno the Battered Bear seemed appropriate. Yet he was good natured and happy to be part of the threesome.

The two younger bears would take turns. Hans would present himself to Bruno, standing with his paws at his sides. The older bear would rise and hug his friend and the two would wrestle, pushing and pulling, fencing with their muzzles. Though twice as large as his partner, Bruno was careful not to overpower him. He would let the smaller bear push him down and onto his back. Supine, he would box lazily with his front paws. Then it would be Fritz's turn.

With a mild south wind blowing, Bruno and the Kids became overheated quickly. They would collapse on the snow and lie there sprawled out like three throw rugs on a waxed floor. A few minutes of play would call for 15 minutes of cooling off. Then the next round would start.

After several hours of play-fighting, the older bear left the game to the younger bears, who were happily sparring like a pair of Olympic hopefuls in training for the Greco-Roman wrestling events. Bruno walked to the crest of the shoreline, where tides had piled up kelp in long drifts. He began digging into the kelp, eating a little now and then like someone sampling tidbits at a salad bar. After excavating a comfortable bed, he curled up in the hole and drifted off into a nap.

In the afternoon, Hans and Fritz found Bruno in his bed, his back and head lightly frosted over with snow. No further introductions were necessary. When Hans stood up to ask for a game, Bruno roused himself like an old pro and joined in again. As the sun set, the contestants were having a great time, flailing away, twisting and shoving in gathering darkness while grinning happily at the joy of it all.

For most people, of course, "hands off!" remains the sensible policy when considering an approach to even such engaging animals as polar bears. An exception to the rule is the case of an experienced guide who recalls his fondness for a mature adult male polar bear that he named Ozzie. The bear came to know him by sight and would trot over to his vehicle whenever he emerged. Ozzie learned the sound of his friend's voice, as well, and would come when called. Ozzie liked to have his ears scratched; he would stand up and turn his head to encourage it. Of the hundreds of wild polar bears with whom the guide had interacted, Ozzie was the only one to show a desire to be touched by humans.

Older bears seem willing to accept the role of teacher or coach in allowing younger bears to practice the fighting skills they will need to fend off competitors and mate successfully with a female.

Once said to be solitary animals, polar bears make friends
with other bears and enjoy hours of play.

Preceding pages: In drifted snow amid a willow thicket, two males practice their fighting skills. Play often takes place between males of different ages, with the older bear taking care not to hurt the younger one.

Above and right: Two bears adopt the classic posture of invitation as they begin a boxing match.

Facing page: Ice piled up along shorelines or pressure ridges offers concealment to bears hunting seals. During winter, bears kill an average of one seal a week, but they increase their take in late spring in anticipation of slow summertime hunting.

Hudson Bay polar bears, marooned on shore in summer, must guard against becoming overheated. Any temperature above freezing is warm to a polar bear; at 70° F, bears can become seriously heat-stressed.

A brilliant sunset silhouettes a polar bear walking across a frozen pond on Cape Churchill.

Taking care not to hurt each other, bears spar with their muz-zles and paws.

"Adult bears, especially the most youthful males among them, play as well. Polar bear zoologists call it play-fighting, and suggest that their games constitute a friendly means of practicing the physical skills a sexually active adult bear needs to compete successfully in the springtime mating wars."

Above: This female will keep her yearling cub with her for another five or six months before driving him away and mating again.

Right: The male yearling cub of this young female polar bear is almost as large as she is, but still depends on his mother for protection from larger bears and help in catching seals.

Right: The nine bears shown socializing in this photograph refute the idea that bears are lonely hermits unwilling to tolerate each other's company. As many as 64 bears have been seen occupying an acre of beach at Cape Churchill.

Following page: After a swim to cool off, a young male shakes his head to clear water from his ears. On this day, water temperature and air temperature are the same: 41° F.